Harm Eden
Copyright © Jennifer Nelson, 2021

ISBN 978-1-946433-77-0
First Edition, First Printing, 2021

Ugly Duckling Presse
The Old American Can Factory
232 Third Street #E-303
Brooklyn, NY 11215
uglyducklingpresse.org

Distributed in the USA by SPD / Small Press Distribution
Distributed in the UK by Inpress Books

Typeset and designed by dourmoose

Printed and bound by McNaughton & Gunn
Covers printed offset by Prestige Printing

The publication of this book was made possible by a grant from the New York State
Council on the Arts with the support of Governor Andrew Cuomo and the New York State
Legislature, along with support from the National Endowment for the Arts and the Robert
Rauschenberg Foundation.

HARM EDEN

Jennifer Nelson

CONTENTS

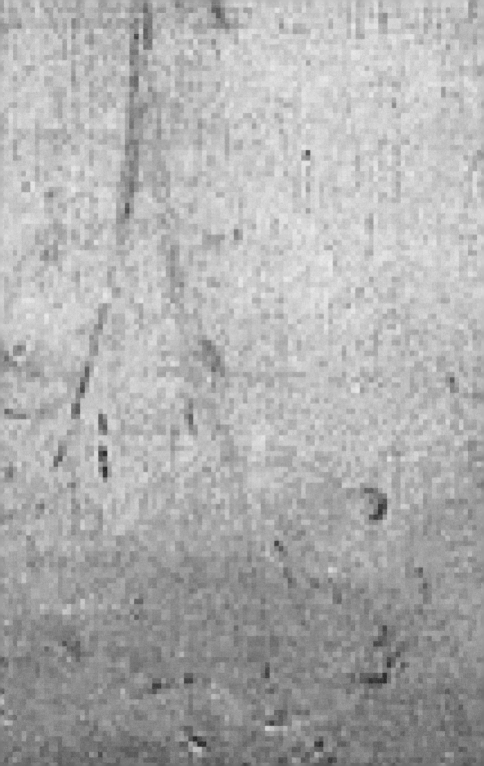

HARM EDEN

INVOCATION TO THE MUSE

Have you ever found yourself
harming the forest
out of rage at your own feet,
the leaves

so dense the wind
brings tones from them,
no sky but sky's gift,
green sifted sun?

Walk with me, o Clio.
I was wrong about your hands.
They are not the hands of death at all.
They are perfect, chubby yet skeletal.

THE RHYME OF THE WESTERN TANAGER

Seagulls are here to talk about death
though death has no continuity
as the glacier of the sky extends
deep north
onto Lake Superior
then east to the St. Lawrence
and skims across the first dead ocean.
Wrong names. The gulls
are forcing us to talk
about death while the rain
flaps its hands
for us all. What is the first question.

Who gave Hector his earring
in the lost tapestry of Troy
that is really Constantinople.
Who misgrieved
one thousand years of Christians
on the Bosporus strait.
The rain flaps its hands.

The first question is what
would you say on the last day of school
if you knew there were nothing else you could learn.
The cars keep sliding
over the ultimatum
abrading it and mudding it
but the line is of course much deeper.

We know birth doesn't make color. Nor is it local.
That patch of yellow

right above the mid-tailed ass
and the sparkling fake
tropic song
have nothing to do with Wisconsin.
A beautiful chain of rings
spills from my embroidered collar.
Garrotte, gallow, guillotine.
The songbirds resettle
without continuity.
The pair of gulls, dawn and night:

I must narrate this perfect person
to whom there is nothing I can give.
Their beautiful jokes about coffins
and claims about honey
the tamer of horses
I must sew into the wall.

Here while the cars stop coming
the concept of audience is a dodge.
Words are dizzy, full not null.
They decorate with silk the empty lodge.

I HOPE TO BE AN UNSETTLER

No land has ever claimed me,
no person, no people, no place.
I am always standing between burials
and the nearest tree
holds all I can know.
At the spring words bubble up
and trickle down in banderoles.
At first I had to read them
till the grass smelled sweet
and the bugs bit home.
Getting old means reading them
while the hill of my choices
grows. At the end of the field
a deer measures the meadow.
She is so small today.
What words can you possibly wear.
What can I bring you, I
so without kin
I have no hands,
no apparatus,
thus offer my persona
as medium,
a wager: assuming
there's something past myself
or perhaps a way the particular dead
with whom I've walked
have shaped me in some unlit land.
What land. I cannot even say it lies
beneath the creek
because the creek can never be mine.
No creek can ever be mine.

I take what I should carry.
There is a clicking sound when I stay still
like a gas stove failing.
I defined by misfire.
I defined by naked love,
love without relation, I
have piled miswords
on your desire. Now
I'm asking for forgiveness. Not
the ordinary kind,
puckered with regret.
I am asking for a kind
of eternal endurance,
like a child who jumps across a chasm
and does not want to jump back.
Keep me clicking, please.
Skimming while the bubbles break my feet.
In the field the deer finds grass
at just her height.
But not because she wants to disappear.
Something's breathing to make those holes
while the woodpecker strikes a pose.
I have to believe the right world follows.
I shout each time it comes
like the sun shouts a highway
over open water,
hoarse and bright and wrong.

I HAVE A SECRET

I have given my life to history,
and I do not care about history. I care about

the deceitful stillness of water
cut off from its home, and the fragility

of skin, all skin,
as the brave interface. I want

to skin the knee of water. I want
to tell you something so true

you sing like legs, carrying
our hopelessly binary meaning

in a third direction.
This is the way night looks

from the top of the Tower of Babel.
On top of the Tower of Babel we've murdered

all possible kinds of building,
all possible kinds of labor,

and every architectural style. We sit there
waiting for night that cannot reach us

or at least mostly doesn't
anymore. It is the most beautiful meaning

I've ever seen or heard

watching you walk your song

back to me on this once
-impossible patio built

on the death of work and suffering
but somehow not of difference.

We kept the curse. We have herb gardens.
I am making you a salad now

of fruit and sinless venison.
Water condenses when it wills

saltlessly out of the eyes
of anyone who agrees.

Time doesn't need sight or detection.
Without them I keep its other name.

LET'S MEAN THE UNIVERSE

what do the stars write all day while the sun
keeps us from reciprocating
I imagine

let's imagine
they're sirens
of an emergency that's time

and though they have taken the solemn
aspect of mute
facts interrupted
at best by dust

it is possible to shift into a faith
that they are blaring
that there is something to be said

intermittently as best
to fuck with mandatory forward
and be ourselves
and by us let's mean the universe

IF SO, WINTER

one night vortex cold
a tree under streetlight
turned to brass tips
like stars
pointed out on an astrolabe

o Aristotle
or my love
the pain is a crown

can't you feel
every resemblance on earth as intended
and therefore vagabond?

RETRIEVAL

some say they remember clear as day
~~but let us pray~~ but when day comes
it's blinding each time
then not, an acclimation
standing in for other acclimations

silence between planes
a long blue descent
snow gusting up
then not

one day instant messenger died

       does it mean
one has grown up
when paradox feels tiresome

think of the sky above the snow

I wanted to contain the outer shape
by hugging it
this was the use of theology
one could hold the incommensurate
by means of love / advanced respect

To the one being quiet
I have asked you to speak
With the life I have hoarded
Kill me if you have to
But don't fuck it up

SCOPOLALIA

From the crispy edges of an old cut flower
to the soft inside

or splitting a bud to flick the pointless
engines of its future, protostigma
skin on ovules

taking on the hypodream
that simulation doesn't matter
unless we fetishize originals, I want
to live somewhere we don't
fetishize originals

by violence if I must

The probability a string
will swing toward one
accident or any other
or configure many
or require another parse
informs the architecture of retrieval

on a planet where very loud thunder
recalls another planet

THE INAUGURAL PRESIDENTIAL LECTURE AT THE
SCHOOL OF THE ART INSTITUTE OF CHICAGO

while we were watching a video
of white cops killing
Black people over and over with a thousand
other humans
in an auditorium another
cop killed another Black
person while Black students
listening prepared to phrase
their questions about triggering
carefully because the video
was by a Black hero while other Black students
backed up the ones who got dismantled
by the hero while a Black
professor challenged the hero
on appropriation respectfully while my hero
fell short of catharsis on a horde
she almost forced to be "American"
while I cried and ignored my colleagues
while I got angry
so many people weren't crying
while I refused
to medicate seek treatment
for being so easily disrupted
while deans mock the hypersensitive
while people fail as people
for watching with straight faces while
literal systematic killing
should dismantle
the fetishization of harm as art
while that sight should

disrupt everyone
while I don't want to be cured
but want to choose disruption
while I want that freedom
another cop shot another
Black non-hero and he died

LETTER TO THE PRESENT

Today I'm writing from
the Ministry of Fire
We've lost our throats here
Trees are bare
In the many
hallways behind us
doors are closing
and echoing down
to you: magistrate,
    what will be your choice?
    An aproned man wears heels and clatters
    Will you meet his flair
or will you retreat to that gray rock
by a non-refundable sea
and say "last stand"
The left hand moves
The right one doesn't
I'm writing because we disagree
about the origins of waves
Limp
as flayed handskins
you do not clap

SO MANY THANKS / HARM EDEN

0

so much supposed to be beautiful's beautiful
only because it's not alive, not

mixed, not the first chimera: world
and outworld
needing each other to stay
young and old, respectively.

tell you the truth
harm's the only garden here
and recovery its asters.
news comes from repeating
knobs of wisteria, oozing
slugs, and cornsilk flies

1

singing upside-down about
Earth's automobiles and jets
to insensible and wild
hydrangeas and osprey.

guillotines chatter in streets
upkept by professional
immigrants, streaming
laundry lines of visas,
left hands raised
and oathing crusade infidelity
under skyscraper chuppahs

melting in terrorist
ecstasy. this is also the museum.

2

running away is not an option.
everyone of course runs
back into the same
elephant working their personal
circus, one ring
closing on the audience.
and the trunk curlicues a note:

maybe we are the entertainment.
if we feed, say, mosquitoes, we should
know this as our particular
effect, in other words, meaning.

olive groves still exist
lined with cats, who
invest in the end of all resources.
value this, purr their tall-tailed
ends, well-licked. what better
reverence to Athena than this

3

auto-immune snake
reclining gently
into its own tail
and forgiving itself its own
nature scale by scale?
all animals self-metaphorize,

animal humans most of all.
listen: every morning
issues its own frequency,
cicada-style. what if
everyone knew their sonic simile

4

as a form of greeting, rubbing
limbs carefully and matching
each oscillation? it'd crowd out silent
xenophobia. sound. the number
2 tells us we should have bypassed

5

Janus by now, and the binary.
every day we survive the US
American blight we plant
new engines for a world

6

jumpstarted past comparatives.
engineers push code back into its own
navel, a spring in itself,
no input. I said this before: imagine
yearning twinned with

love satisfied. a listserv that only
I check to which everyone subscribes.

[interlude: the Sibyl]

come to think of it
how could our paradise
run its self-destruction and not
intermit?
suffering, like
the tide,
intercepts itself
nonstop. there is no final
exhibition of capital

but home, which flickers
relentless as a fly. Harm
Eden pays its bill and
tips, then
totters down the strip.

7

June arrives. July. elsewhere
oil rigs stamp deeper and harder and more.
ransom is called on utopia.
diamonds found on Saturn
array themselves against its ice. how will we
networks of gardens

collaborate across texts?
over eons of lakes
little melodies persist, cob,
ibis, pigeon, a chord like a fist. a dead
nightingale falls off our wrists.

IN VIRUS'T-// SPRING

We'd gotten nowhere with theory.

Every time we imagined brushing our teeth we remembered the difference
between a razorblade and a hair.

There was a debate whether sculptural niches were windows. Did the
sculpture park make fields into windows. Jar in Tennessee. World Picture.
So on.

Never think the birds sing maliciously at our graves. They are just hungry.

THE HISTORY OF MEDICINE

For those who don't know Vesalius: Vesalius
invented remote teaching
with unethical human subjects
and the premise of virtuality.
Woodcuts aren't holograms
but good enough. Good.
Now imagine Vesalius
touching your baby.
He talks a lot about it.
Especially the skull
from which he draws conclusions
about softness
reminds him of rain on Vesuvius,
he writes in his diary
which will not survive.
Rain on Vesuvius before
or after an eruption?
asks a later entry.
While in quarantine Vesalius
writes letters to his past.
The past as best as he and we
can reconstruct it answers
during. Think of smoke
bushes on lava
and ashballs freighted with wet.
Ongoing death by suffocation
steamed by unrocked rock.
No one wants Vesalius
to touch their infant's head
but he does, over millennia
and miles that aren't his. Creeper caress

like a Care react in sacred time
while in Wisconsin
over fields of unborn corn
five hawks arrive for slaughter.

KEEP IN MIND THE FOREST IS JUST
OUTSIDE THE FORMER MALL

Today there was the bear.

We ran it so today there was the bear.

We ran it so I was hugging myself on the forest floor on pine needles that were red dead but bendable. The graze against my forehead, the activated scent in my nose when my 90s Timbs crushed the needles. Like that.

Not a lot of context or sounds of approach. Just suddenly bear. Coming over me.

And what did I have. Like a stick or something. I stabbed right away, hard. We ran it so I tried to lever the bear off me with the force of my body's momentum like in a martial arts movie.

No. But the stick moved. It jerked awkwardly inside the body of the bear
.

We ran it so the bear didn't move. So I could just test the feeling of the stick going up and down, left and right. Like a chopstick in meat.

The recommendation was for everyone to cut their hair. Some say there's no point in running the model out past two years. But when you do, the curve becomes irrelevant, and the suggestion is to cut your hair.

CONSERVATION PROJECT REPORT, MARCH 2020

It was uncomfortable at first to watch the Raphaels being sprayed down with actual COVID-19. Through my hazmat visor, smeared on the inside, if I'm honest, with my own mascara, I watched the slime re-oil Raphael's oils. For a moment they looked re-workable.

Then my discomfort turned altogether. I noticed it first in the Oddi altarpiece's predella, in the Annunciation panel. The decay in the lapis lazuli pigments, everyone's favorite nod to global trade's role in the art of Western genius—wow. The decay was … reversing, it seemed at first. The darkness to which our ultramarine blue, obtained through hard labor in what is now Afghanistan, so often succumbed over the centuries here lightened under the virus.

All I remember next was an odd black, purple, and brown fire, if you can imagine a fire being those colors. It was those colors. Warm even through the suit, the fire first spread down to the floor where the Madonna sat in her once-darkened-blue gown (at that point on fire). Then the flames surrounded the tiles. Obedient to the rules of perspective, the fire shot back past the columns and into the infinite distance.

The problem is this: must the fire not also have shot forward? Look carefully around. Use the enclosed poll to grieve your hands.

WHILE ORPHEUS WAS IN THE UNDERWORLD

Tell me the secret of the world jewel
I said horizontal to Monteverdi
in a red cavern picking
rain from machines

Like a screensaver or pong I bounced
slowly because with love
unable to accept this life
a weight in the back of my pelvis
neither fertile nor waste
another pain
anchoring my predictable sway

algorithmic but in such a way
I would not return for generations
to this place and time and pose

of which

some are more the fulcrum
of the hourglass than others

The more they tried to flee from [ ]
the more [ ] swallowed them

SQUIRRELS

if I think I've survived enough it's time to start
doing the thing I survived for
casting
the last leaves' glitter
into another creature's nest

I woke up in the middle of the night
and went to transcribe my recurring dream
when Isaac was born

the dream is something like:
I'm live-testing a simulation
and meanwhile must suppress critiques
in order to survive
in order to deliver them

I want to ask Gustav
to let me watch
his snuffing since
he would have once been into that
but I can tell dying makes him not

to survive the parameters of this world
but recall the roads of the one we want
in the cruddy petrichor
the world where it's safe
to give a world to everyone

HUBIRD

no one is reading   no one is thinking
no one is singing   the flight path is sinking
the white sky is rumbling   the side roads are crumbling
over the speed bumps   under the cars
the jetghouls mourn   the dead dinosaurs
if I'm too slow   the jetghouls mourn
and one choked bird   makes tweet on the hour
how to explain this   when caring kills "art"
poor Paradise Lost   so misunderstood
evil is hardly   less boring than good
the gray sky is gurgling   the ceiling fan wood
since Satan's not Satan   Satan is us
the only method   that works till the end
is to honor what's human   to wait for the bird

REHORSAL

the standing fan   and the ceiling fan
pair like sea   and contraband
with yesterday's punch   and yesterday's pirate
yesterday's love   and the oven pilot
I feel the trees   prepare for winter
stretching their bark   like a fisted glove
at the equinox   where light disrobes
the pediments   and caulked alcoves
the treetops and   the winched windows
hunched over boxes   dripping with wind
words start to loosen   and soften their ends
the balding tree   nibbles its gold
this is why   winter is old
not the birth of a savior   bleached hay underneath
the sidewalk rotting   with blotted brown leaf
fall disinters winter   fall is tomb soil
the scarecrow's stuffing   live organs' foil
Itay would say   fall is baroque
the moment of brilliance   the moment of choke
but autumn comes after   it commemorates kill
it mocks preservation   it will not keep still
when the wind in Chicago   tickles its leaves
and the sidestreet shadows   start their long shrug
like a horse at its bridle   hating its driver
it shivers sideways   till the bit tugs
then knows enough   to start a good trot
there is no survivor   but death's proud mascot

BARBITTUARY

inspired by Aliyah Khan

when Ashbery died   I felt the carapace
of History rise   and fall round my sensorium
that lusty breath   sugary thighs
arms controlled   as a hammersmith's
its thumbless fist   pushed the corpse aside
and dripped fresh lymph   at this podium:
fire behind golfers   buildings on their knees
water in the airports   salamandered trees
crawling in the office   of Aung San Suu Kyi
before Puerto Rico   a partial list
mixed from the slides   that History clicked
Barbuda I fold   into St. Kitt's
the typical fail   of an "American" ditz
who's wanted to shelter   whom ICE would deport
but actually never   opens the door
since at the door   might be death
(who we heard in line three   and saw at the top)
why not today   I heard History say
a whole island gone beach   with humans still on it
alongside thousands   of Rohingya Muslims
provides the topic   of History's speech
as the route of the storm   takes the slavers' form
behold in disasters   the endgame of masters

THE (RACIAL-INDUSTRIAL-)COMPLEX
SATIRE OF FORLUNA LE FEY

defer your catharsis   please   please
as the sun hides behind   the moon's pocked knees
as soil dries in the pot   as leaves unwind
if the moon's orbit rots   rejecting the Earth
then at the least   when floodwaters rise
their tithe to old Luna   will piddle and fail
for what it's worth   my you includes me
with major exceptions   but I've lived off sums
from a violent culture   that bankrupts the frail
I have suggestions   since we're all adults
don't giggle at suffering   honor the strange
burn down your own kingdom   burn your blank page
only thereafter   comes heart-y laughter
but I fear the beast   that wheels out Fortuna
till you white and white-passing   persecuted as Parsis
fill your own prisons   you'll never parse this

ALLEGALOREY

at the Field Museum

at the end of the jar   toward the face of the prisoner
taken in war   by a long-dead soldier
with spacer'd ears   with colonial tears
from bowls with insects   mashed into meal
and watered to red   to cochineal
the museum wandered   the exhibits changed
the updates squandered   on "eskimo" pain
I dreamed of an igloo   to house my end
I heated a poker   to break my leg
when I read the oracle   fragged into my bone
I learned my error   no one dies alone
so off in the tundra   of algorithnet
I packed my paint treacle   and drank from art sweat
after I'd rambled   for hours four score
I managed to find you   Museum Galore
your skin it had aged well   your face it was red
not a natural color   something stretched until dead
you drew out the joker   then gave me the pack
but I wouldn't read it   I wanted you back
and so you forgave me   for hacking your trough
for of the old "freedom"   we'd both had enough
then we lay down   our bank accounts open
and called the most delicate   jackals to glutton
and as we lay prone   as we lay token
our enemies moaned   their currency broken
and from the exhibits   the artworks pranced
they wafted their air   out past their labels
and moved out to where   the dream world was stable
where the dream world was stable   the Yuit throve
the Tlingit the Haida   Inupiat droves

Athabascans and Aleuts   and that's just Alaska
the rest of the northwest   exhibit hall
put on its boots   and danced its own thrall
thus thrall was danced   till each process disabled
itself and its cost   no convenient fable
this is unstory   this is your boast
this is how you   lose alle   get glory

TWILIGHT IN THE NEW LIFE

The thing that changes
is that hope ends

said a monk
applying mascara

Hope ends and work is left
On one side of the diptych

appears a herd of buffalo
Poussined; on the other

you must see yourself again
in thick clouds

forced out
after many years in the league

in the thick clouds now
the star of many seasons

THAT SMILE

Male Questioner: is there ever a reason you'd have different footnotes
                bottlecaps
                on the same poem?

Swashbuckler: well there are many different versions of the same poem
                and these will have different bottlecaps
                on different words

I wanted to say I would live
to defend difference over and over

but I don't like representations of should

as a ragged dustfroth sways
and notifies no spider

too broken to sustain this love
I've tried to save the satellites

as an old woman tests her face
looking back on the computer

COMPASSION! FOR HUMANS!

persuasion is a long game
reliant on erotic
nostalgia, and I
welcome the return
of the long day, birds
on wires shiny
through winter scum
hopping, a video
of a girl beneath rubble
I cannot finish, clicking
nor turn on the sound
imagining instead
a pbs
special on archaeology
a careful brush, an ostrakon
a line of dusty children
with potsherds on their brows
modeling art's collapse
of time: I have no room
for affect except empathy
the best thought driven
by emotion always
which is why men fear it
we all know we're best when angry
from love
and thinking through it
many seasons angry from love
and thinking through it

WE, WILL ACT, ON LOVE!

I saw my theologian friend at the vigil
and noticed holes in him, a patchy render

A painting that tells you it's painted and real
      both, a lot

      Do I want
people to dream as if in life or should
we always

      bury cows

      I am referring to the news of the badger
        I saw the night of another war
        who did that, buried cows

How many protections one has
so one doesn't feel the benefit
from other people's dying

      Why log in
        if not for the bio
        politics of feeling? Oh

      Bark on a tree like earplug crust

The badger buries the cow
and saves us from its maggots

Groom oneself
for exploitation

perhaps

      but
the church has never been vestigial
I almost grieved sound's artificial
fall into meaning
waiting for planes coming in off the lake
to talk about morning
          Instead
no past but what we make it, game
The earplugs of the inner ear
      the one that hears old time
      tend to expand but may grow brittle
An athlete pours evoo on her skin
      that smells of sun
      and digs up a strigil

        sing it here
      the church has never been vestigial

WELL BTWS

In the hour before the puking tram
at the end of the barchipelago
I discovered the definition of magic
and riding the old-fashioned cigarettes
texted the people who'd need it

Just as in the Tower of Babel
what cannot be painted
       transfers into poiesis
           Every form of making
in material and labor
       suspends its bad
Why bad Bruegel must we list the cranes
the breaking and boil
the ladders at all
      a material
      a material
Must we divvy humans one per task, and leave
unions and syndicals
just as invisible
as pied communities of words?

__[no, thank you]__ / hindi, po! /
I want not the building that ends as a bowl
the stadium of staged capital
with traditional distance-colors brought
from pastoral to urban
the high horizon crammed with dismal roads

I want the other tower, the one that touched God
so could not be taken

So, Bruegel, go:

How many did you paint this way?
Whose hubris did you try to check?

Well btdubs

magic is critique without distance
and action is its side effect

MY PLAN

A real life hunt for the golden fleece

preserved somewhere in Siberia

undertaken

by the world's richest men and / or

their proxies, is thwarted

by a shifting location

The dark protagonist Medea

the quantum art historian

leads them through the chains

of old portraits one

after another

into

individual suitable punishments

for particular betrayals of humanity

Though human she

maintains an ever-changing

poison word

CRANACH'S *ST. CATHERINE ALTAR*

the storm seems inescapable
because inspired by a wheel
into spokes of fire and hail

if I could have good nature
follow me or have the winds
support my command

I'd ask for this:
muddy clouds on local castles
cut off in the corner

if I must die I'd ask:
let light fall upon my killer
and let him be a jester

our bodies
crammed hail and fire
spokes and hub

a fragment of a rim and axel
with innocent humans
cranked past hell

if I have to die
between the jester's smirk
and the damned

feel the storm flutter flower-bows
on his coat and the wind
straight away from you

hair and feathers and flames
away from you
they're all blown back

you do not imagine your impact
all paintings take a constant
hit from the future

like all survivors
I am calm when I feel it
blowing back

AFTERLIFE OF THE CHRISTIAN SOLDIER

the artists went embedded
with probably the generals
prepared for the overlook
not to project the ancient
Mediterranean but to stretch
the limit of literal corpses: I'm guessing
weapons weren't included
even in the strictest painting
of resurrection in the flesh
no one pops up in the front
spraying dirt with a halberd
ready to stab the angel or demon
allotted: so-called punching up
or am I wrong to google the hope
of war unending war after death

LIKENESS BEATS SAMENESS

who is right, and are we ever
alone correctly

the particulates, anguilliform
through the raisined cellulose of leaves

I left a garlic in my bag and let it
ride asleep the train

a green tongue
a spring I slept and dried

THE FINALE

Dawn builds across a snowing
then lights a wire where
a squirrel circuses, fat

All the questions I get
are about photography
against the enduring

appeal of art deco
hieratic old flat
how Europe

recovered its own origins
Most people have an accurate story
that ancestors traveled

and stopped: this dream
was about a contest
that's always stopping

over the unborn crocuses
Is the perfect allegory of survival
a prize always analogous

to life? The car as life, the one
hundred thousand dollars, the lifetime
supply of tools for the art

that won one the contest
to start? The special
power of mimesis

is its recasting
the process of revelation
as already foregone: I mean

maybe one can't anymore wait
for the squirrels to be seeable
let alone the flowers

Maybe we're supposed to be afraid
to see it wrong
like dawn through a six-day cloud

though only dawn through a six-day cloud
can prove the blizzard is real
and not just interference

ergo you are alive

MY CANDIDATES

in the tent near Tropicália
in the eighteen hundredth
childhood on the edge
of the canal in old Kreuzberg the branches
amid the red lights on the chained
platforms in the water the gray
green light of the Love Parade
at dusk in the Tiergarten
in the notebook left on the boulevard
between my grainy toes
on the fortress wall outside Manila
over the shanty valleyway
under the rain on Lake Michigan
in front of the flopping
fish beneath the thunder
around the fishermen with teeth
behind the cat attacking
the glass walls after the chipmunk
after the first mouse died
after I threw it out the window
on the front façade before
I thought I could talk to you
in the gardens of Córdoba
before the lightning startled the cats
while I was imagining no god
and failing before I had truly
inhabited my emptiness in
the wake of [ ] when I clicked
all the way down to the pending
friend request from my dead lover
when the radiators came back on

in Chicago at last for the end
of my life under the thunder
during a trick of summer
between the piles of online shopping
strapped into the headphones
of the show above the mismatched
blisters on my feet one
permanently blooded
since I had not in
so long looked someone in the eye
and touched them simultaneously
with soda crackling in the can
on the coaster on the
table on the wooden boards on the
rotten wooden boards
above the aging
sorority tenants above the concrete
over the pipes and the laundry
under the thunder
in Uptown Chicago I bent
the flowers in my knees I folded up
deep flowers in my knees
sweet potatoes in my pelvis
do you mourn bones
while tulips curl up in the reddish
black wet air

ALONGSIDE THE MARKETING

ALLEGORY OF INFORMATION QUALITY

I'm responsible for potatoes.

Huge quantities of potatoes are being harvested and brought to storage facilities by enslaved people. The soundtrack is ethnomusically informed jazz.

I'm supposed to be counting the eyes on the potatoes, but the enslaved people have huge quotas, so they never stop moving. Them or the potatoes.

ALLEGORY OF THE CAVE

Instead, I explain both sides of the argument about why it's important to know who is making the jazz.

This method of counting feels similar to the boneless method of painting in the oeuvre of Yun Shouping or Xu Xi.

Boneless painting is best for poetry, I lie to the students. Do not try to tell a story with it.

SIMULATION OF THE FREE ENERGY PRINCIPLE 1

Once upon a time eye-sized flakes of bread fell out of the sky. It is not coincidental that a human bite is the size of a human eye.

For the smaller particulates associated with fire, one website recommends water and ginger administered to the gut rather than the lungs.

Then, one day, a mysterious warrior arrived, in search of a dragon.

WHAT VERY WIDE EYES YOU HAVE

Dear Signor de' Medici, I hope the curtain bugs come in heavy. Hungry is a given.

I'm writing because there isn't enough rain in the sky to account for the missing emotions. Please advise.

In the laboratory we keep the women awake for days at a time. We call the result of their yawning "Wind Machine," and paint accordingly. Yours, Zeuxis Kaizhi

ALLEGORY OF PREPARING TO HAVE BEEN

Dear Qianlong Emperor, Chundi, etc., etc., each woman must be provided
one pearl sewn at the neck to secure them to the silk. This will prevent
them from telling the future.

Please find awaiting your seal the dossier on world dragons.

And several designs for mills. And the housing of the workers. And
the sewage levees. The boycott is holding strong at the border. Yours,
Parrhasius Scardanelli

ALLEGORY OF FOGHORNS

(a) Each Dragon shall file publicly on the Internet in consultation with an Art Historian high-resolution ("hi-res") images and extensive verbal descriptions of each item in its Hoard.

(b) Thereafter, individuals with impaired memory shall have access to a long-durée experience of said items' simulated presence.

(c) Any Dragon who violates this provision shall burn potatoes for no more than twenty hours per violation per year of violation.

NO ROADS LEAD TO ROME

Rain is saltier near the ocean.

In a Song copy of Han Huang's *Boy with Water Buffalo* the creatures curl up accordingly.

My explanation leaves out which specific ethnic group in fact created the jazz. The rock is whorled and its perforations circular. On the tree some leaves survive.

SIMULATION OF THE FREE ENERGY PRINCIPLE 2(.0)

When the pages were found the necessary tests were done on the wormholes. . . . Yes. I don't mean in the papers themselves but in the woodblocks that touched them back then.

You have read Crowley's argument that Parrhasius ate paper.

No, that does not explain how either of them got here. . . . No, there are no bones on this table. . . . Oh. Thank you. It was hard to avoid them.

ALLEGORY OF UNRECONSTRUCTION

Everyone comes to examine the dreadhole at least once. Some multiple times.

Who can blame them? King David sings so beautifully from underground. It's how anyone knows where to harrow.

If you stand on the inner crust of the earth noon comes when the sun is at your nadir. Surely, Sire, you can see how there is no point in counting anymore. Release me.

ALLEGORY OF DEL *.*

I lied. Even the skeleton of the dragon will not suffice unless I leash it.

All roads lead to home. The free landscape exists only at the deepest core of the interior. In Zhou Wenju's famous *Double Screen* only the serving women can touch it. And we don't.

Compliance is futile. Settings • Main Menu • Retry

IT REALLY IS THE END

I wanted to resist
apocalypse trends
but the sun at the brim

of the skyline
seen from a garden across the street
sings red light,

the streets turned crenels
for nightrise: I imagine
my body dropping onto it,

this great city
at the edge of the sea
and my flesh

parking the towers' sturdy
spikes against me,
packing the city in.

Sure, why not
cuddle Chicago one last time
and curve along the lakeshore trail

and admit I have grown fat
and capable
of administering the entire Earth

after years of ordinary weariness,
like women at a "witch"es' sabbath
drawing from the Renaissance

let the moon do their backs and bellies
like wind and come
from the grit of the chalk

thick at their necks, the many hands
at work, eyes
drawn down to crumpled paper

worn from use, words undead.
Is that the mane of a goat
at my feet when I lean

back and let the sun
flinch behind the tall
buildings of Michigan Avenue?

As the sculpture garden grows cold
and dark I am warm.
If only I were the end of the world.

DISBAND THE POLICE

At the lake after more protests
I was thinking bits of time
could be bosons of light
but we have to fight
the myth of inevitable nature
especially human since now
we can fall asleep only
with billionaires breathing on the phone
like God
underneath each screen
small iridescent murders
made regular to look like depth
connect us on Earth
while a gray
blue heron shakes its fringe
its light blue shoulder
fringe and twitches
its wingtip its
pinion before
taking off a-skim upon
the lake meniscus
and torn against that heron
foot a-tracing
ripples onto algae
the surface
will not bear more weight
recalling
the parable walking on water
its silver wrinkles traveling
moiré like words
rotated in time

Roman Ducksworth, Jr.

we could also imagine

Benjamin Brown

bits of light

James Earl Green

were bosons of time

Philip Lafayette Gibbs

that suppressed directions of time

Delano Herman Middleton

drive all light

Henry Ezekial Smith

but what if we agreed to stop

Samuel Ephesians Hammond, Jr.

separating world and sky

Edward Garner

power from its bearer

Samuel Shepherd

or the heron

Robert Hall

life from value

Matthew Johnson, known as "Peanut"

IN WHICH TOSHIRO MIFUNE AND
TATSUYA NAKADAI NEVER FIGHT

the faces of samurai
up close in the 60s
twitch
like finches

when I went into the Vineyard Sound I felt an old
distaste for the slime on the smooth
rocks at the surf and pressed
the balls of my feet past it

the seaweed
out in the water wrapping round my limbs
and torso like a jellyfish
as I swam to a scummy
inflatable raft
and back to the broken-up
breakwater or wayward jetty

and back

I ask about a relation
between portrait and close-up
in painting from the Quattrocento
or early Byzantine mosaic
or the lead-up to ukiyo-e

think of poems obsessed with the ocean
or how automatons have seemed
wrong yet delicious
when humans could not record in time

this technology nostalgia
drives the samurai flickering
from portrait to close-up
by the force of emotion
from woodcut into cinema

not that their feelings could translate wood
but that they carry the forest with them
already processed by our cuts

the ocean tastes delicious
and I forgot to drink it
thinking later it's as good as alive
and carries only change
which makes it the greatest
classic killer

MY NAME MEANS INFILTRATION

The truth is I *am* from Atlantis.
My intellect has destroyed the world.
The real problem is that my apocalypse
cannot end.

Morning still feels
like plastic in the sky.
The ruin of modernism
is what makes a city charming

especially against a twilight
the hue of a gas leak tamed.
I go up and down the towers
several times a day and never

stretch so my legs turn into
crystal. A cheap trick, but one
we Atlanteans employ
to help conspiracists.

God bless the simple dreamers.
We put the temple of the Sibyl
on top of the capital's hill.
On a clear day you can pee or cry

directly on Christ. We are so efficient
waste flows backwards into Nazareth,
into Chaldaea, writing your Horus name
into the mantle of the Earth.

I could have said there's something untouched
we must still save, and sell some line
of no return. But Atlantis is always returning.
Atlantis means harm in the language of gods.

BERRY POOP

If we keep the Earth habitable
then Jean can live forever:
the able-bodied one, with her trowel
off the seashell path
teaching us to pull
tiger lily stems.

Get rid of all this damage, the proteins
tangling the vineyards, the morning
scum on the trees, the scrap
snaking the lawns
into second nature:
the parody of the first
that kills the audience.

I reject the terraform. Instead
let's pluck the weights
inside our hips and wait
for consonance. Is that sexy?

What comes out of a bear
is not in its image
nor in the image of the planet
nor in the image of God.

How many times have her bare feet
gnarled before my eyes
on slate plates
with grass flirting
like low tide?

I know what time looks like.
The seahawk holds the fish
and the electric wire fries.

HERCULES FURENTES

It was actually before
Hercules went mad that he
needed to get past Atlas
Mountain to get the Geryon
cattle (of the sun) so he
tore Atlas apart so the
water burst from Ocean
and became the inland sea
aka Mediterranean

                that was

all procedural
When I look down on the Chicago River
or the quarries beside it
toward O'Hare
it's easier to see a monster tear
the land and water down
than think of decisions
and wages (garbage)

                just as

if on a nondestroyed Earth the future
entities are astronauts they'll
imagine myth on a mono/cosmic scale
unless it flips and a swarm
of lights appears and children think
the stars are workers every
light a thousand
workers each
swirl a common concert

I

blame Hercules the entity
the literal historical Hercules
We are crazy • we are dangerous

THE BIRD

pain is often a reality effect
I mean
sometimes there's no real
referent in the world left
for a feeling, just the sense

that this is real, a stone dove floating
above a stone virgin and
realer than the virgin (which
is what the paint announces
if believed)

in my lifelong quest against modernist purity
I hunted down the neurons
in all the presumed modes
of trapping sense
and organizing it

I ducked beneath the dry
wingpit of the angel
I squeezed my thick dark blood
and reflected what stood in front of me
as dead

I I said said
that projection jection of statues atyous
is the form form of learning earning
we have to have to curate careful heirfully
the incarnation nation of ghosts love ghosts

ACKNOWLEDGMENTS

Thanks to *AIR TALK*, *BathHouse*, *Bone Bouquet*, *MAKE Magazine*, *Palimpsest*, *A Perfect Vacuum*, *Pinwheel*, *Social Text*, and *Versal* for publishing several of these poems, often in slightly different forms.